Cats Being DICKS

BY JULIE KITZES

Cats Being Dicks, A Funny Adult Coloring Book for Cat Lovers ©2022
Julie Kitzes

All rights reserved.

No part of this book may be reproduced or transmitted in any form or by any means, electronic or mechanical, including photocopying, recording or by any information storage and retrieval system, without written permission from the author/artist. You may not reprint, resell or distribute the contents of this book without express written permission from the author/artist.

All violations will be remedied with legal action and justice will be sought to the maximum penalty allowable by law in the State in which the original purchaser resides.

Cover Art and Illustrations: Julie Kitzes

Printed by: Kindle Direct Publishing

ISBN-13: 979-8831976212

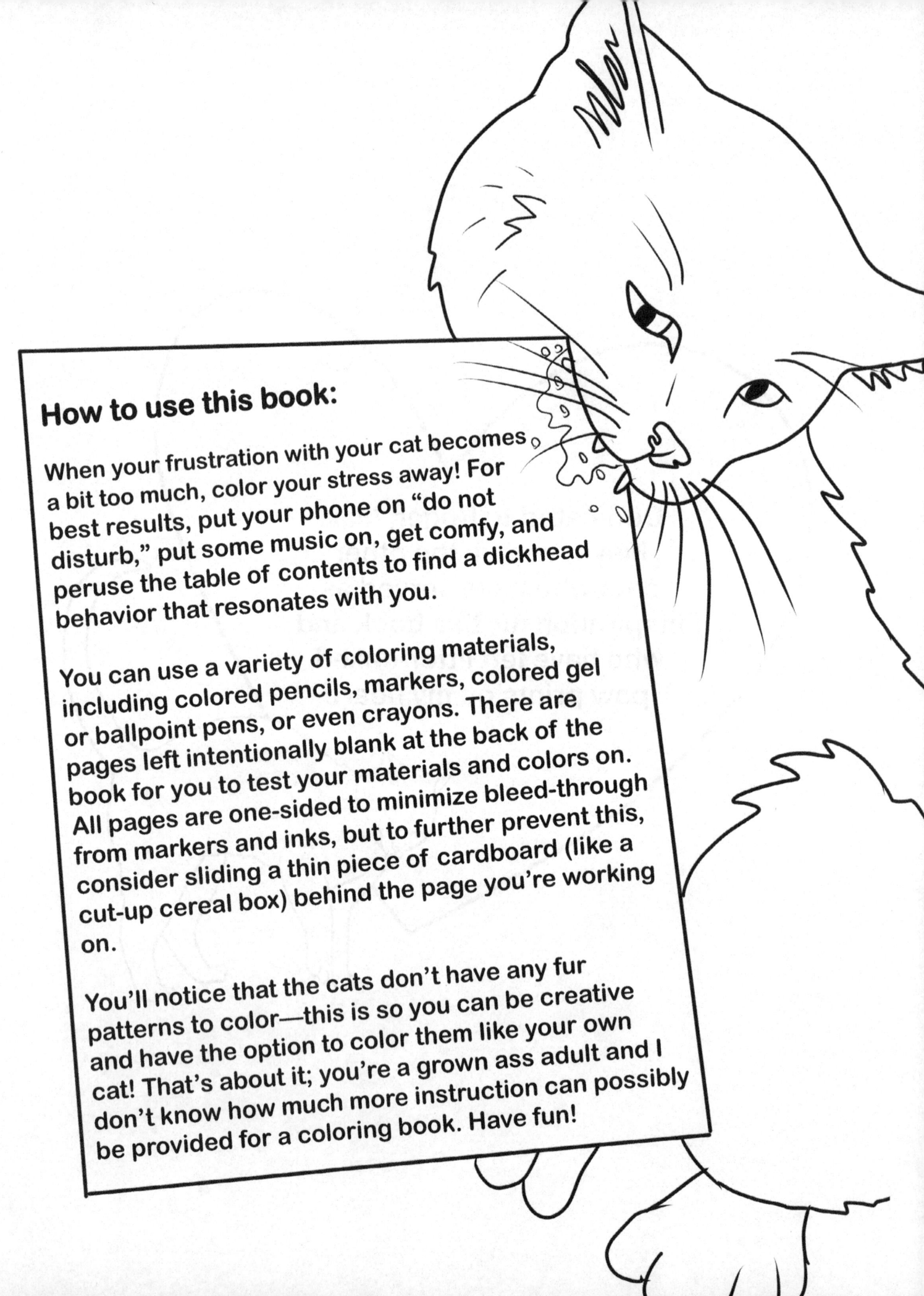

How to use this book:

When your frustration with your cat becomes a bit too much, color your stress away! For best results, put your phone on "do not disturb," put some music on, get comfy, and peruse the table of contents to find a dickhead behavior that resonates with you.

You can use a variety of coloring materials, including colored pencils, markers, colored gel or ballpoint pens, or even crayons. There are pages left intentionally blank at the back of the book for you to test your materials and colors on. All pages are one-sided to minimize bleed-through from markers and inks, but to further prevent this, consider sliding a thin piece of cardboard (like a cut-up cereal box) behind the page you're working on.

You'll notice that the cats don't have any fur patterns to color—this is so you can be creative and have the option to color them like your own cat! That's about it; you're a grown ass adult and I don't know how much more instruction can possibly be provided for a coloring book. Have fun!

For an additional free printable coloring page, visit the link below and subscribe with your email to learn about future books and projects.

https://www.juliekitzes.com/catsbeingdicks

Share your colored creations on Instagram with the hashtag #catsbeingdicks or post your images with your Amazon review.

Contents

When your cat is a dick and pukes on your pillow. 9

When your cat attempts murder by attacking your feet on stairs . . . 11

When your cat is a dick and tries to steal food off your plate 13

When your cat is a dick and uses your closet like a climbing wall. . . 15

When your cat is a dick and shreds your important documents 17

When your cat is a pyromaniac and tries to burn the house down . . 19

When your cat is a dick and co-opts your hobbies 21

When your cat is a dick and knocks your vase off the table 23

When your cat stares at the corner and freaks you the fuck out. . . . 25

When your cat is a dick and breaks your blinds 27

When your cat is a dick and annoyingly discovers the door stop . . . 29

When your cat is a dick and climbs up the curtains 31

When your cat is a dick and spills water on your laptop 33

When your cat is a dick and shreds all your toilet paper 35

When your cat is a dick and eats your houseplants 37

When your cat is a dick and claws up your sofa 39

When your cat is a dick and tracks paint all over your house 41

When your cat is a dick and shits right next to the litter box 43

When your cat is a dick and threatens to break your phone 45

When your cat is a dick and starts yowling at the crack of dawn . . . 47

When your cat is a dick and somehow sits on your laptop screen . . 49

When your cat is a dick and sits on your pizza 51

When your cat is a dick and licks its ass on the dinner table. 53

When your cat is a dick and makes room for itself in the pantry. . . . 55

When your cat is a dick and makes room for itself in your dresser. . 57

When your cat is a dick and steals your dog's bed. 59

When your cat is a dick and plays with the gross trash 61

When your cat is a dick to your other cat. 63

When your cat is a dick and bats at your wall art 65

When your cat is a complete dick but you love them anyway 67

About the Illustrator. 69

Coming Soon 70

Blank pages to test your coloring materials 71

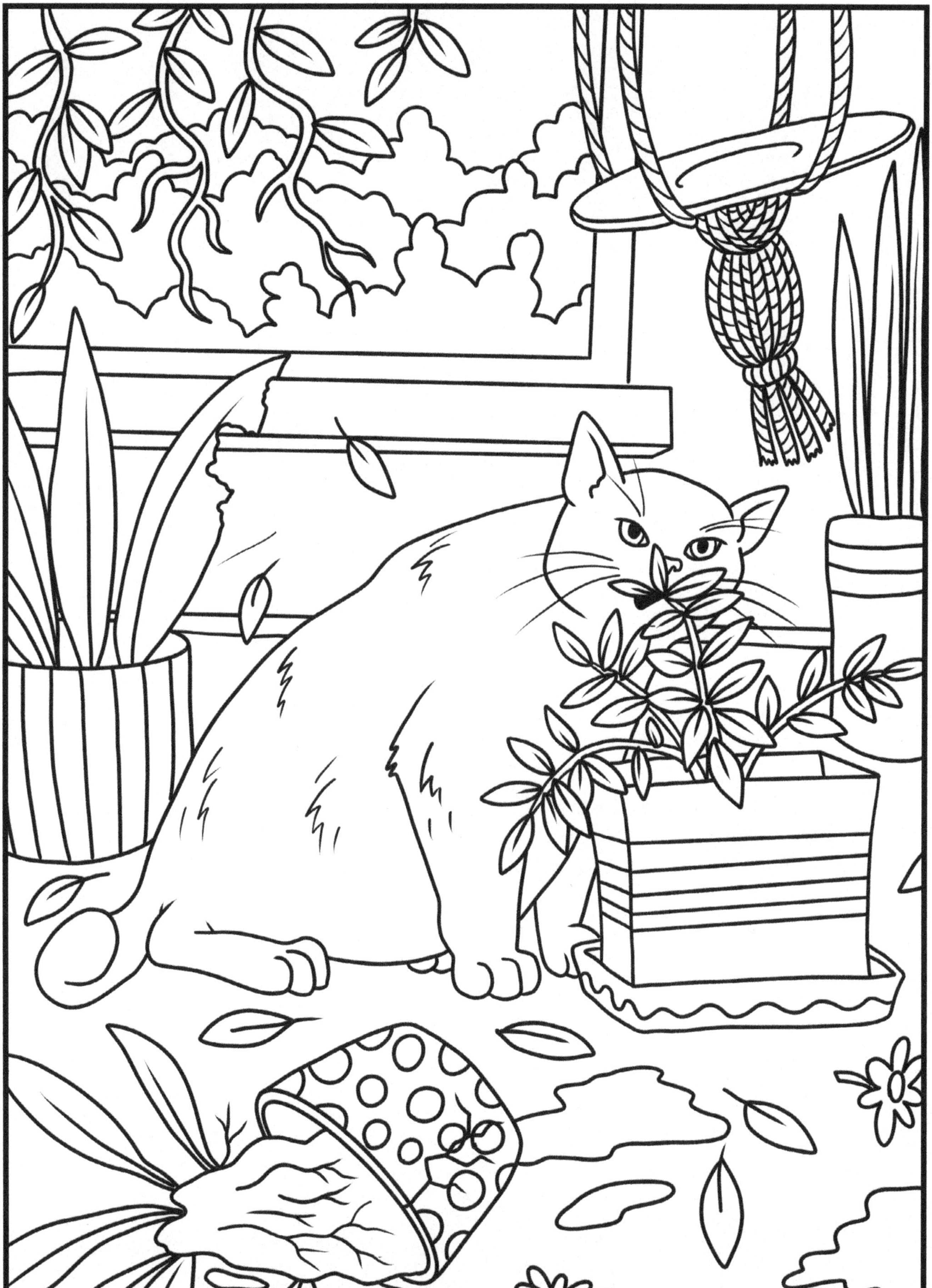

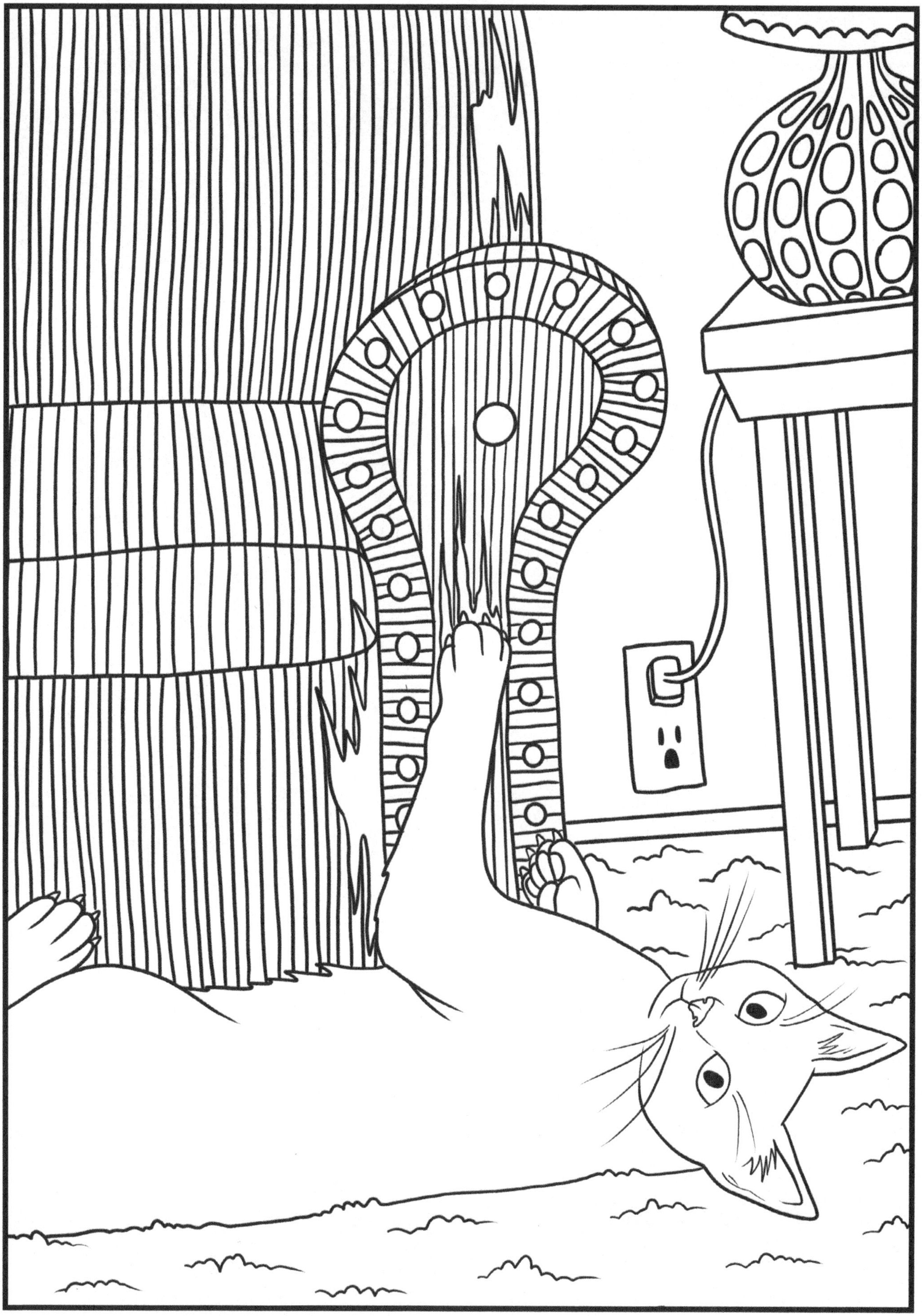

40

41

43

44

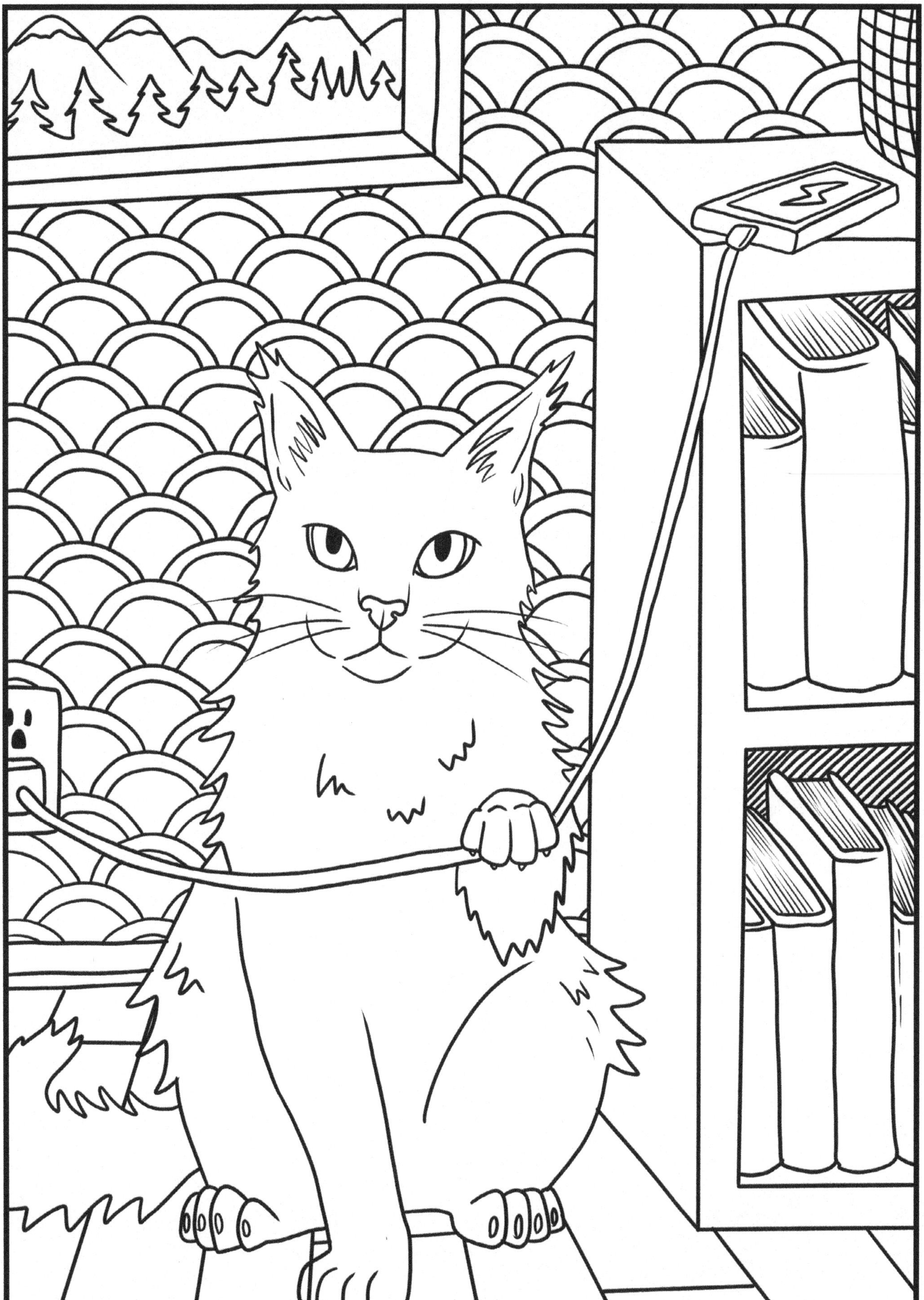

47

48

49

50

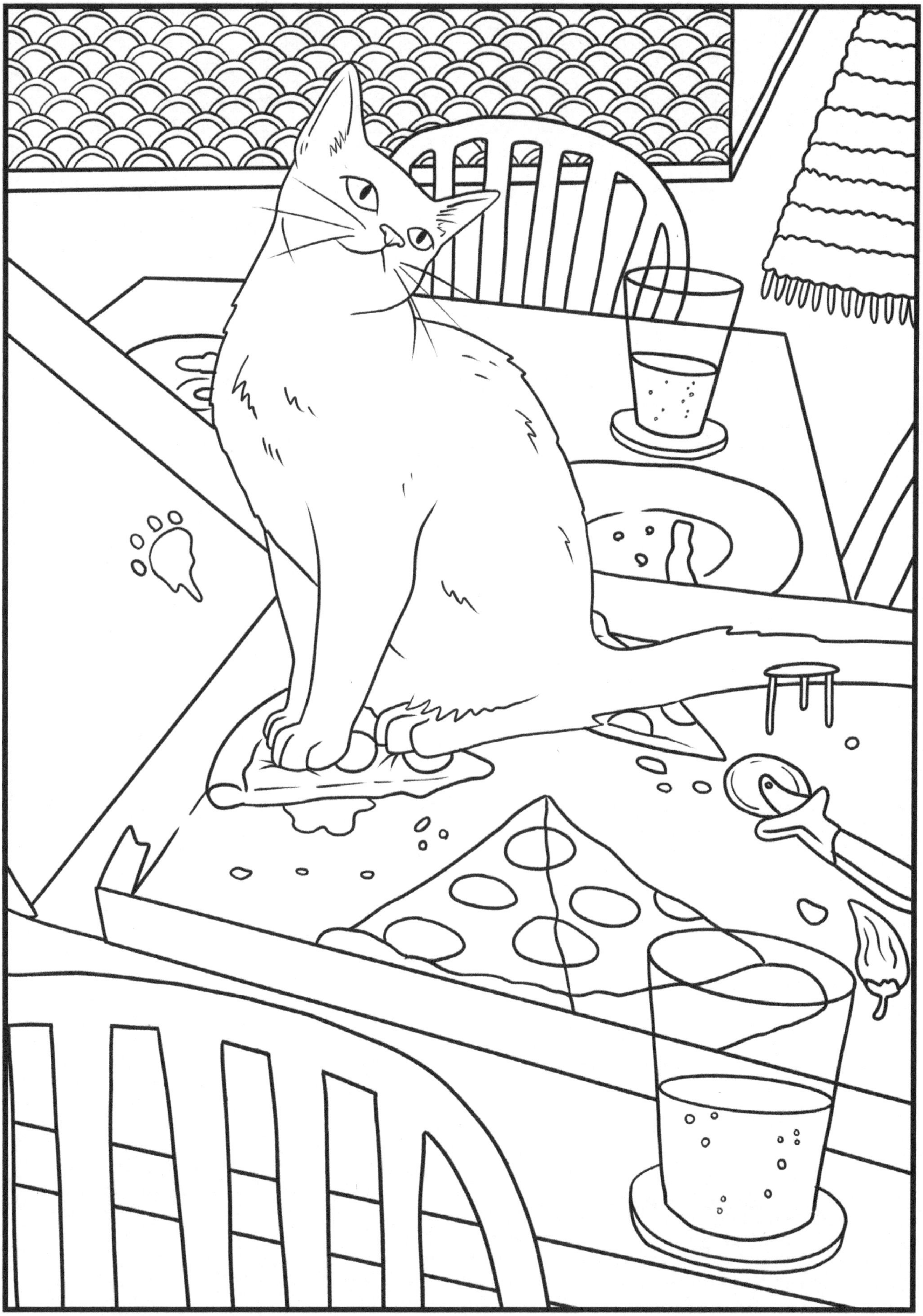

53

54

55

57

58

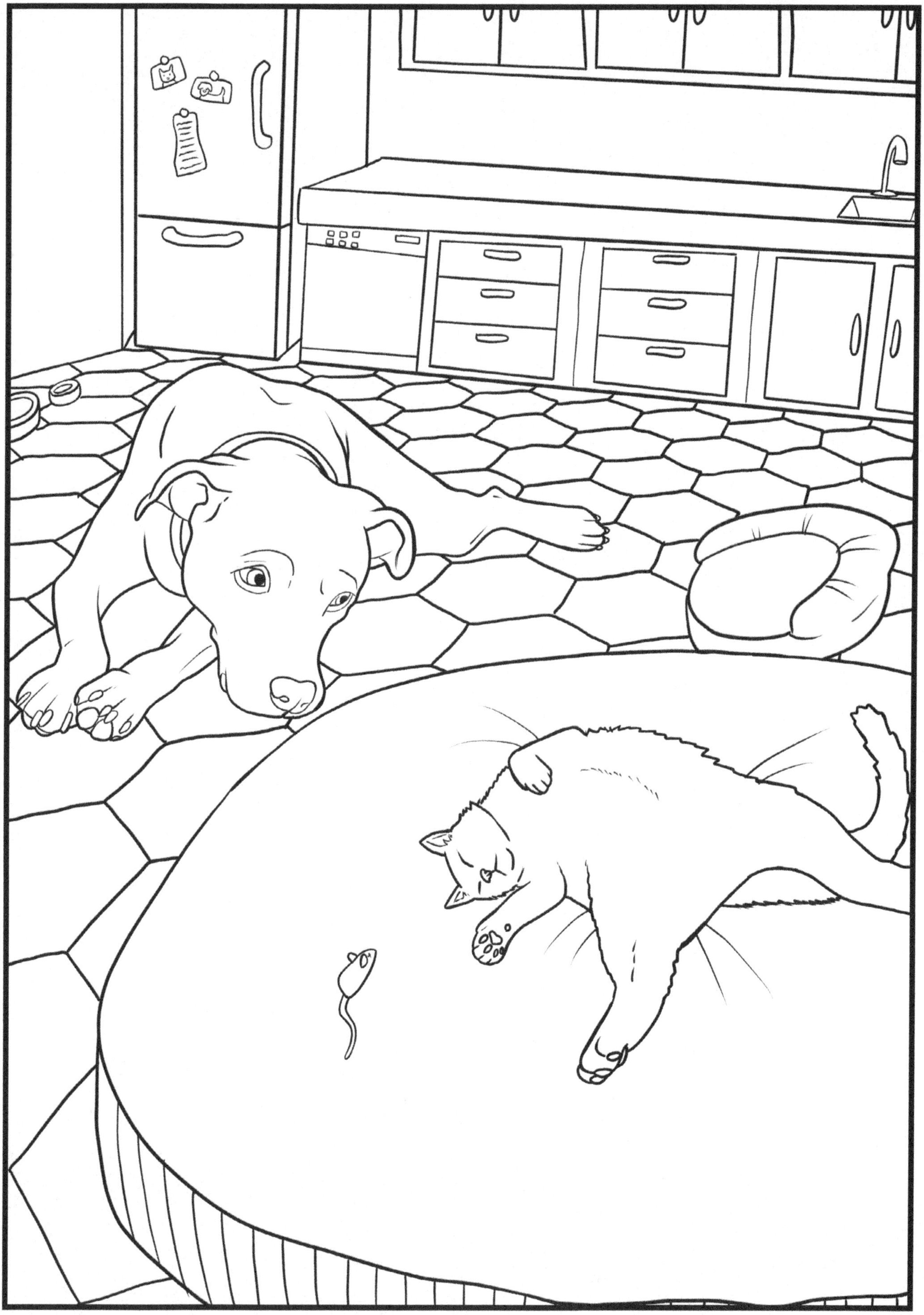

61

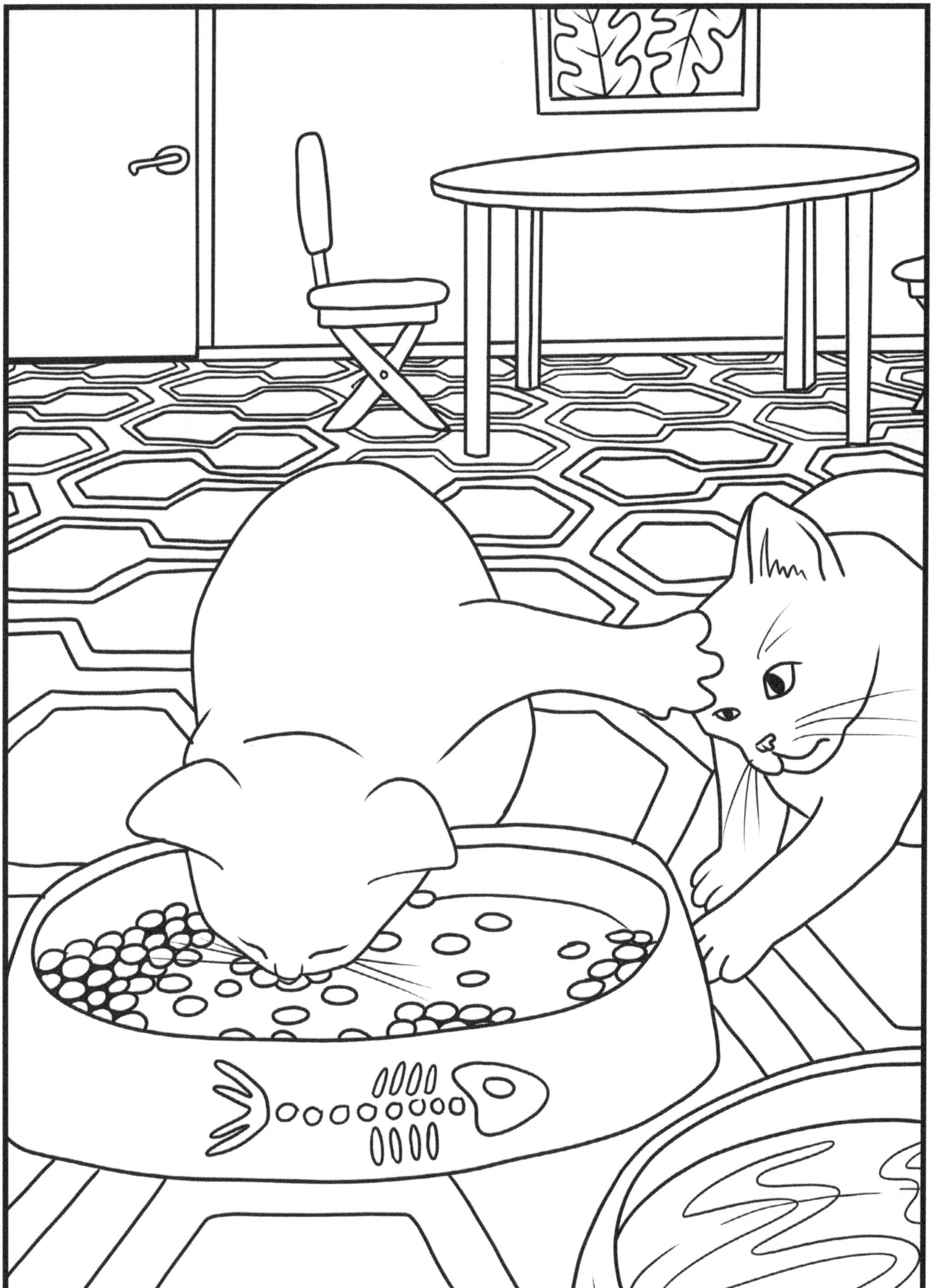

64

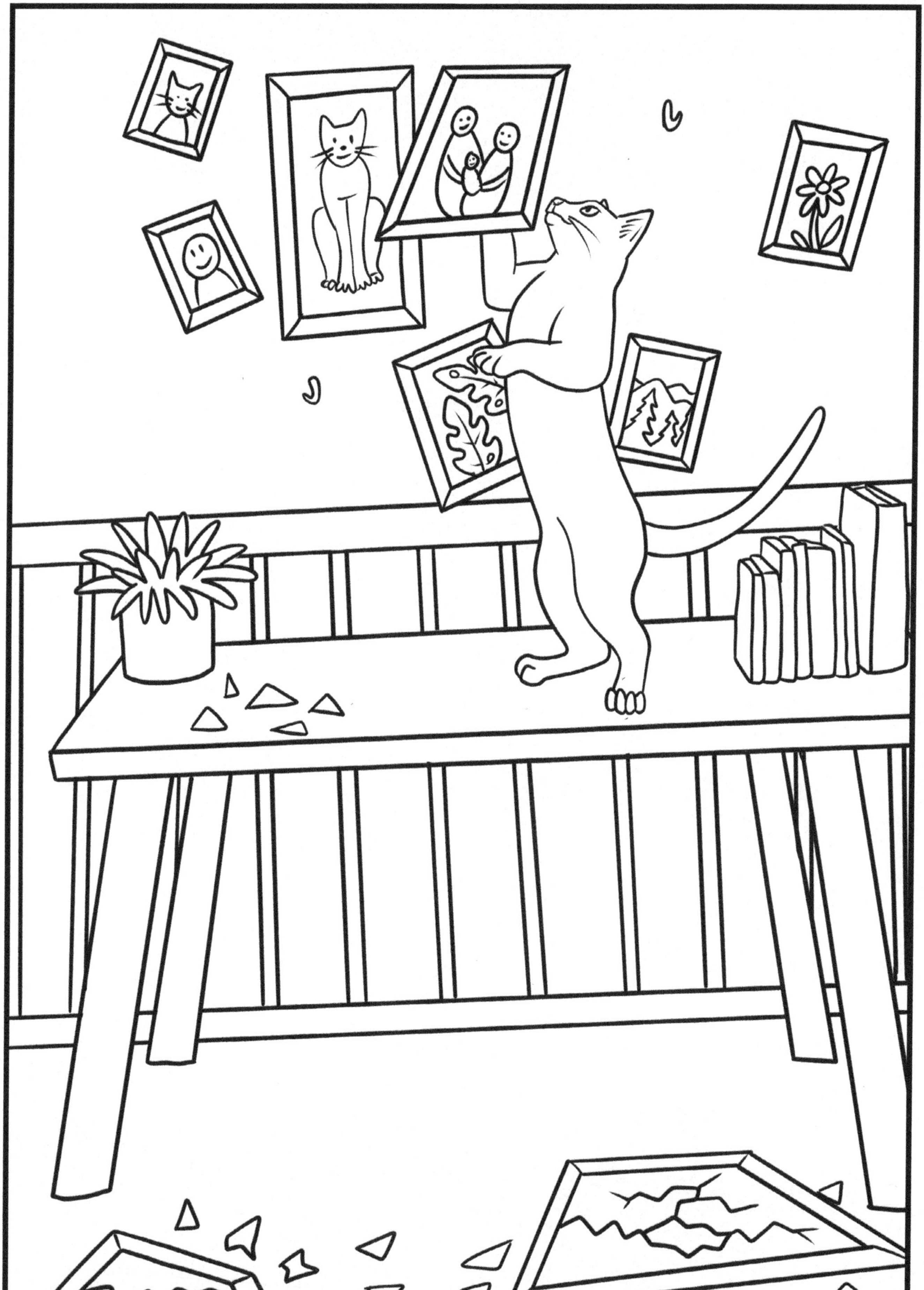

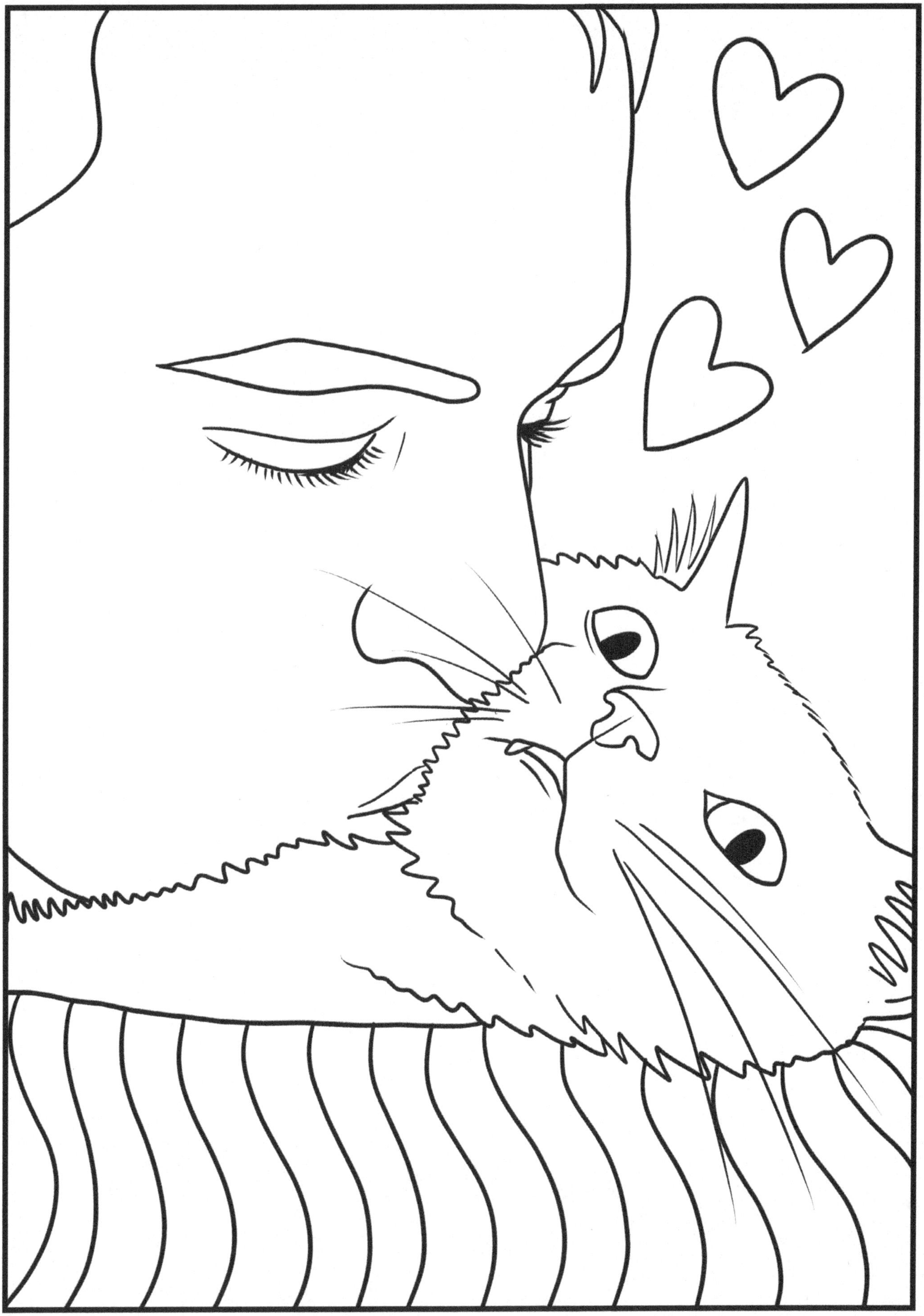

About the Illustrator:

Julie Kitzes is an illustrator and fine artist residing in Denver, Colorado, with her husband and their willful (read: dickhead) ginger tabby, Roger.

Julie considers herself somewhat of a cat aficionado since she's not only been a lifelong cat mom but was also a veterinary technician for over ten years before starting her career as an artist. She's also worked in pet hotels, shelters, and a grooming salon, so she's seen it all when it comes to humorous pet behaviors and has inside knowledge of some very specific ways that cats can be dicks.

Though she loves all animals, cats have always held a special spot in her heart. Despite the fact that cats can be dicks at times, she maintains that they're the most special, clever, loving, and genuine creatures out there.

When she's not making coloring books or smothering her cat with unwanted affection, you can find Julie drawing pet portraits for her clients and pursuing all sorts of other creative endeavors, from needlepoint to public murals.

To see more of Julie's work, visit www.juliekitzes.com, and follow her on social media @juliekitzes.

Coming Soon...

Test your coloring materials here!

Made in the USA
Coppell, TX
17 December 2024